ART
Around the World

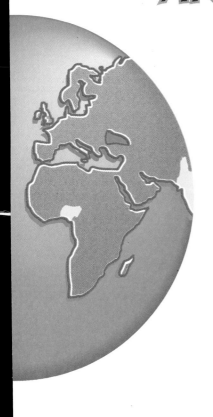

Heather Leonard

Photo Credits

Tony Stone Images/David Tejada, cover.

Tony Stone Images/Oliver Benn, page 6.

Werner Forman Archive/Smithsonian Institution, page 8.

The Hutchison Library, page 10.

Michael Holford, page 12.

Werner Forman Archive, page 14.

Tony Stone Images/Penny Tweedie, page 16.

Bruce Coleman Ltd/Neil McAllister, page 18.

ZEFA, page 20.

All other photographs by Rupert Horrox.

Text for pages 16 to 17 by Penny Stevenson.

Hand modelling by Lisa Melotti.

Discovery World:

Art Around the World

©1998 Rigby

a division of Reed Elsevier Inc.

500 Coventry Lane

Crystal Lake, IL 60014

02 01 00 99 98

10 9 8 7 6 5 4 3 2 1

Printed in the United States of America

ISBN 0-7635-2352-6

Visit Rigby's Education Station® on the World Wide Web at http://www.rigby.com

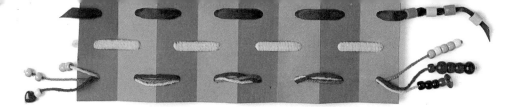

Contents

Rigby

Arts and Crafts

There are many different types of arts and crafts. A craft is a skill which people can learn. It is often useful or decorative, such as making a pot or dyeing cloth. Art is a way of telling people our ideas, thoughts, and feelings, such as making paintings or telling stories with puppets. This book tells you about eight different types of arts and crafts.

People do different types of arts and crafts in different parts of the world. This book tells you where in the world you might find someone doing each type of art and craft. Most of them are done in other parts of the world too.

Weaving

A woman weaving fabric in South America

Weaving is lacing threads together. The threads go under and over each other to form a pattern. The woven threads make a fabric or cloth. The fabric can be used for clothing or decoration.

How you can do it

You will need: thin cardboard or tagboard, hole punch, ribbon, string, yarn, beads, buttons, shells.

1 Fold the cardboard five times, like a fan.

2 Use the hole punch to make holes along the middle of the cardboard.

3 Unfold the cardboard and weave ribbon, string, or yarn through the holes.

4 Glue or tie some beads, buttons, or shells on the ends.

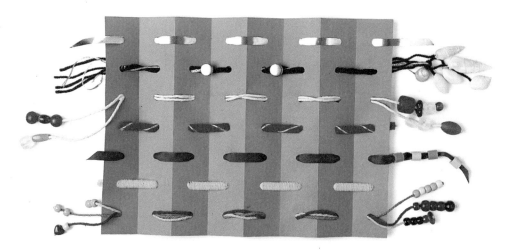

Masks

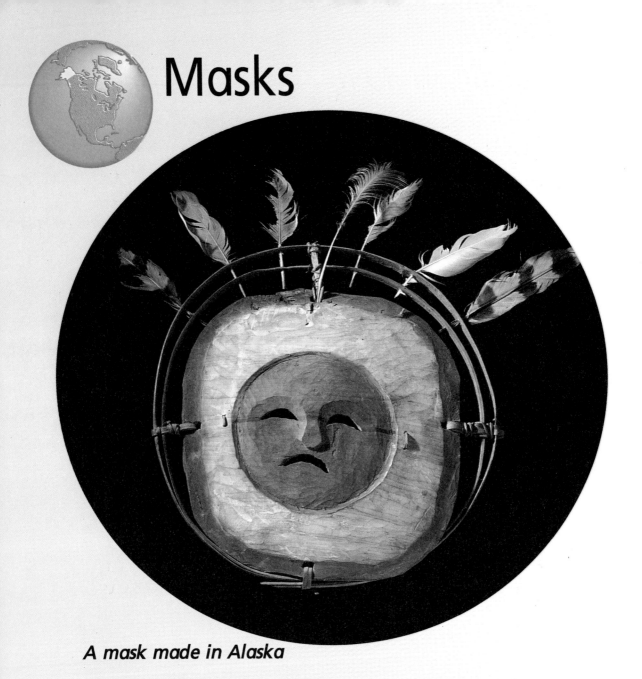

A mask made in Alaska

Masks are pictures of animals and people.
People wear them over their faces. Some masks
are worn to celebrate special occasions. Some
masks are used to tell stories. They can be
decorated with lots of things.

How you can do it

You will need: pencil, cardboard, scissors, tape, long stick, glue, feathers, seeds, leaves, beads, buttons.

1 Draw a large circle on a piece of cardboard and cut it out.

2 Carefully make two small holes in the cardboard for the eyes.

3 Tape a long stick to the back of the cardboard, half way down.

4 Decorate your mask.

Dyeing

A man dyeing fabric in Nigeria

Dyeing is staining fabric with colors. Fabric is dipped in a colored liquid. The liquid is called a dye. Some dyes are made from plants. The dyed fabric can be used to make clothing.

How you can do it

You will need: apron, newspaper, tissue paper, 2 different food colorings, water, 2 bowls.

1 Add a drop of food coloring to each of the bowls of water.

2 Fold the tissue paper in half, then in half three more times.

3 Dip the corners of the folded paper into the bowls of water.

4 Let the paper dry and then unfold it to see the pattern.

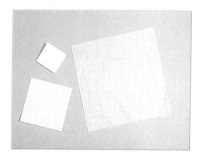

Patchwork

A patchwork quilt made in the United States

A patchwork is made by sewing lots of small pieces of fabric together. The small pieces are different colors and patterns. They are put together to make a larger pattern. Some patchworks are made into quilts.

How you can do it

You will need: some old pieces of fabric, scissors, glue, buttons, beads, ribbons.

1 Carefully cut the pieces of fabric into small squares, all the same size.

2 Glue the squares onto a larger piece of fabric to make one large patchwork.

3 Decorate your finished patchwork.

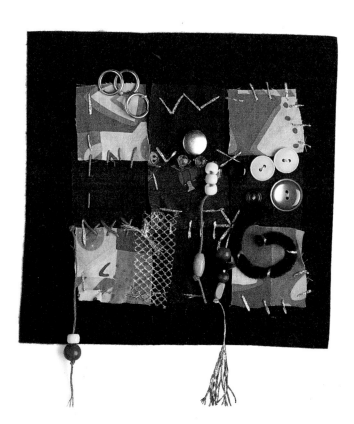

Puppets

Puppets made in Java

Some puppets are 3-D images of people or animals which are moved by hand. They can be held and moved with sticks. Puppets can be used to tell stories. Some puppets can make shadows on a screen.

How you can do it

You will need: pencil, cardboard, scissors, paper fastener, tape, 2 long sticks.

1. Think of an animal shape.

2. Choose which piece of the animal you want to move. This could be the head or tail.

3. Draw the two separate parts on a piece of cardboard.

4. Cut them out and use a paper fastener to put the two parts together.

5. Tape a stick to the back of each part.

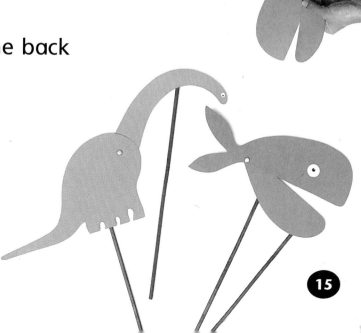

Bark Painting

A man painting on bark in Australia

Australian Aborigines paint patterns on bark cut from trees. They paint with red, brown, and yellow dyes. They also use charcoal (burnt wood) and white clay. Most of their pictures tell stories.

How you can do it

You will need: black paper, red, brown, yellow, and white pastels, chalks, or crayons.

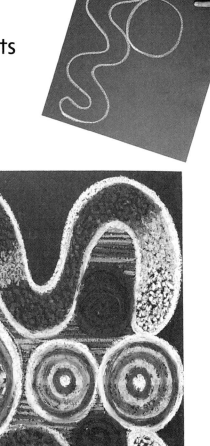

1 Use a piece of black paper instead of bark.

2 Draw patterns of lines and dots on the black paper using the pastels, chalks, or crayons.

Printing

A man block printing fabric in India

Printing is pressing a stamp onto fabric or paper. Patterns are cut into pieces of wood or rubber. This makes a stamp. The stamp is dipped into ink. It is then pressed onto fabric or paper.

How you can do it

You will need: apron, newspaper, scissors, sponges, paint, saucers.

1 Cut the sponges into different shapes.

2 Pour some paint into the saucers.

3 Press a sponge into the paint.

4 Press the sponge onto the paper. You can make lots of patterns using different shapes and colors.

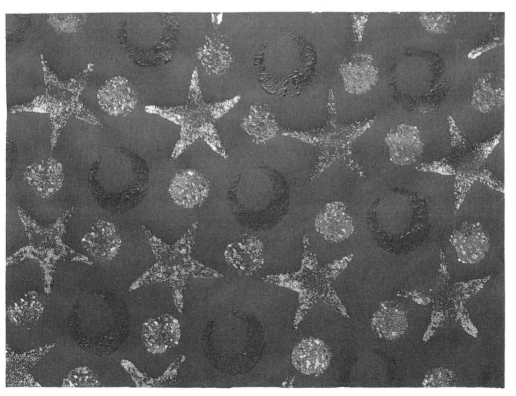

Origami

Origami cranes made in Japan

Origami is folding paper into objects or shapes. The paper is not cut or glued.

How you can do it

You will need: a square piece of paper.

1 Fold the paper diagonally in half.

2 Follow the folds shown in the pictures.

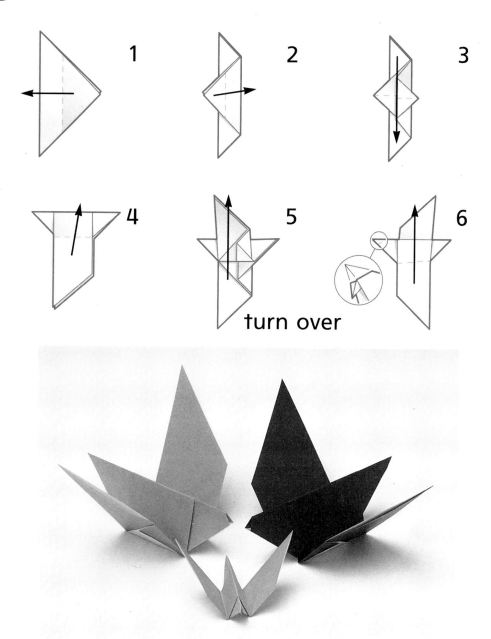

1

2

3

4

5

turn over

6

Arts and Crafts Chart

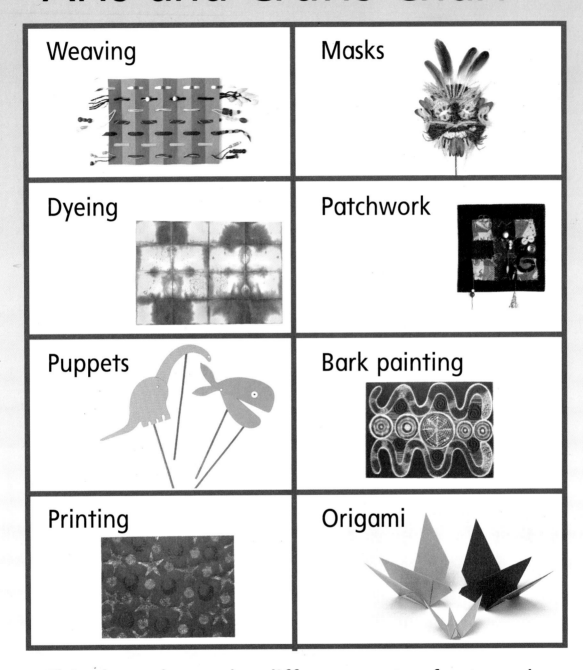

Weaving	Masks
Dyeing	Patchwork
Puppets	Bark painting
Printing	Origami

This chart shows the different sorts of arts and crafts in this book. Can you remember where in the world they are practised?

Glossary

Aborigine

a member of the native people of Australia

art

a skill of making things such as paintings or masks that tell other people our ideas, thoughts, or feelings

craft

a skill of making things which are useful or decorative such as weaving cloth or sewing a quilt

crane

a tall wading bird

decorate

to add things that make an object beautiful

lacing

to pass threads through

pattern

a design that can be repeated

quilt

a bed cover of two layers of cloth with padding in-between

Index